Pugh Finan

Finding Freedom in Finances:
A 21-Day Devotional

To Darcy,

Thank you for being such an
amazing friend. I am so glad
you have been added to my life.
I pray this blesses you and
your family.   Start Now!
                      Heb. 12:11
                      Latrisa Pugh

By Latrisa Pugh

Thank you for beginning, or continuing, your Financial Freedom Journey with Pugh Financial Coaching! This devotional is intended to be an interactive resource for your planting and growth. If you have any questions, feedback, or suggestions on how to improve the guide, please feel free to email us

pughfinancialcoaching@gmail.com

Published By EvyDani Books, LLC
Edited by Windy Goodloe, Nzadi Amistad Editing and Writing Services

Unless otherwise noted, scriptures are taken from the NEW KING JAMES VERSION (NKJV): Scripture taken from the NEW KING JAMES VERSION®. Copyright© 1982 by Thomas Nelson, Inc. Used by permission. All rights reserved.

Scriptures marked NIV are taken from the NEW INTERNATIONAL VERSION (NIV): Scripture taken from THE HOLY BIBLE, NEW INTERNATIONAL VERSION ®. Copyright© 1973, 1978, 1984, 2011 by Biblica, Inc.™. Used by permission of Zondervan

ISBN 978-0-9989945-6-7

Printed in the USA

DEDICATION

I dedicate this book to my friend Danielle, a true fighter who has shown me in the last two years what it really means to have faith and how to get back up again after falling. Although you are no longer with us, your love for life will always be present with me. Thank you for letting me know early on that I am a part of your family. Your friendship and support meant the world to me. I love you and thank you so much for being my friend.

To my nieces, nephews, and goddaughter, you mean the world to me. I pray that you will not have to go through the same struggles. Let my mistakes be your lessons.

To my mom, dad, and sisters. Thank you for never thinking I was weird and not keeping me in a box. Your support means everything.

To Clarke County, my home. I have never been ashamed of where I was raised. All the lessons learned from GHES, WHMS, and CCHS are things that makes me proud. I hope you are proud of me, too.

To my cousin/sister, Dani B. You sure know how to push a person. Thank you for telling me to "just write it already."

To my future family, I am striving to become a better person for you. My journey is for you.

TABLE OF CONTENTS

Learn to live the best version of your life!

www.PughFC.com

FOREWORD

I began my career in the financial industry in 1975 as a banker and retired forty years later as a college professor of personal financial planning. In all that time, I saw the America's economy, and that of the world, go from bang to bust and back again many times. Yet the individual sense of financial well-being has not ebbed and flowed in lockstep with these economic times. Most of those with whom I interacted have felt a persistent lack of confidence in their ability to set and reach monetary goals.

In my years of working to enrich and educate the financial lives of those I have served, one truism is evident: We humans dread discussing financial matters, procrastinate when making financial decisions, and generally view our capabilities as inadequate and not worth spending effort to acquire. We tend to believe we have no control over our own financial well-being which leads us to give up the quest quickly. In good economic times or bad, we can easily convince ourselves we were not born with "the money management gene." But in reality, that mindset is a cop-out.

Unlike almost all other life skills, we did not master money management at an early age. We spend all our youth learning soft and hard skills that enable us to become productive, salary earning members of society. We easily learn early on how to successfully navigate complex social interactions. We learn how to behave in public, develop a sense of responsibility, embrace a strong moral character, choose friends, honor our parents, live by high ethical standards, choose a new career path, and so on. Life goes something like this: start a job, get paid money, spend that money, and theoretically save some of that money for later.

1

Simply making money through work does not automatically ensure financial security. For most people, the steps involved in mastering personal financial skills were not discussed at home, in school classrooms, or during gatherings with friends. In short, no one ever told us what to do or how to do it! Despite the lack of experience or education, the basics of personal finance are just as basic and easy to learn and use.

In *Finding Freedom in Finances*, Latrisa Pugh gives you the tools you will need to conquer your fears about money management. Written in a straightforward, easy-to-understand style, she shows you concrete, tangible ways to turn your money anxieties into a confident walk along God's path.

Jan L. Brakefield, M.S., CFP®

Assistant Professor Emeritus

The University of Alabama

WELCOME

My growth in my personal relationship with God has had a direct impact on my finances. When I began to understand that my financial decisions impact my worship, I began to think twice about how I was using my financial resources. My goal is simple — to help you reach your financial goals while simultaneously helping you develop a closer relationship with God.

This book contains daily devotionals, including scripture and related commentary. This resource will serve as a guide. It requires you to take an honest look at how you manage your personal finances. It is my hope that you will complete these first few days with an increasing desire to align your finances with the will of God. I hope that you are equipped with more tools to help you view and work on your finances. This isn't just a devotional. It is a workbook, a guide, to get you and your family pointed in the right financial direction. I pray that it is as much of a blessing to you as it has been to me.

Welcome to the first days of your Financial Freedom Journey!

A good person leaves an inheritance for their children's children, but a sinner's wealth is stored up for the righteous.

Proverbs 13:22

DAY 1: TRUSTING GOD'S WAY

Trust in the Lord with all of your heart and lean not on your own understanding; in all your ways submit to him, and he will make your paths straight.

Proverbs 3:5-6

If you were born and raised in the church, you have heard this scripture thousands of times. If you are a new Christian, you have probably heard it, at least, a hundred. The word *trust* is a small but powerful word. Two definitions, according to *Webster's Dictionary,* are:

> 1) a charge or duty imposed in faith or confidence or as a condition of some relationship;

> 2) something committed or entrusted to one to be used or cared for in the interest of another.

As we go on this journey, you will have to decide if you are ready to have faith in someone else to help you make your financial decisions. You will have to remove self and focus on something that is greater than you. At the end of this journey, it is my hope that you will approach the same level of trust, regarding your finances, as you do in knowing the ground isn't going to crumble underneath you.

I challenge you to allow the Holy Spirit to enter your heart where it relates to your finances. Sometimes, as Christians, we only let God in on the things where we are comfortable. It is easy to sing "I give myself away," or repeat the commandments "thou shall not" or avoid (insert your personal comfort level convictions). All means everything. Jesus thrives when we are uncomfortable. When we are weak, he is strong (2 Corinthians 12:10).

So let's get uncomfortable and change our lives for the better!

Trusting God's Way

Reflection Question:

What has prevented you from trusting God or someone else in your past?

What have you excluded from "all things"?

Action Item:

Jot down one financial decision you are proud of and one that you are not proud of.

Prayer:

Lord, help me to identify the areas that I have not trusted you in, regarding my finances. I welcome you into my heart and finances. In Jesus' name, Amen.

DAY 2: ASSIGNING VALUE

But store up for yourselves treasures in heaven, where moths and vermin do not destroy, and where thieves do not break in and steal. For where your treasure is, there your heart will be also.

Matthew 6:20-21 (NIV)

"Where your treasure is there your heart is also." You may have heard this phrase many times as well, but what does it really mean? Without overcomplicating it, the simplest way to approach this is by asking: What do you spend most of your day thinking about or doing? Whatever that thing is, it is what you are prioritizing in your life. This may possibly be a gut check, pat on the back, or "I really don't know." Either way, each moment of your day, you decide what you are going to focus your energy on. Decide today to make decisions that will not only help you today but for a lifetime. We will learn more about this later.

Trisa's Truth:

In college, I was in a town that had a Wendy's. I was so excited. I grew up in a small town, so we only had it on rare occasions. I happened to pull my bank statement and saw that, in one month, I'd spent $100 at Wendy's! I was in shock! I did not know anything about finances then, but I gave up Wendy's for Lent that year. This moment was the beginning of a change in my financial habits.

Assigning Value

Reflection Question:

Why did you start reading this book?

Action Items:

- Write down the most important things in your life, according to your time and bank statement.
- Compare this list with the list of things you speak as most valuable.

Prayer:

God, help me to see what I value in my life. Allow me to understand that the decisions I make now can determine what I am able to do later. In Jesus' name, Amen.

DAY 3: TRANSFORMING THE MIND

Do not conform to the pattern of this world, but be transformed by the renewing of your mind. Then you will be able to test and approve what God's will is--his good, pleasing and perfect will.

Romans 12:2

Have you ever tried to start a new habit? I'm not talking about something huge. It can be as simple as "I am going to make up my bed every morning" or "I will eat out only two times per week." Making that change requires a different process than anything you have done in the past. It is a natural tendency to continue to do what we are accustomed to doing. But when it comes to change, you have to do things outside of your comfort zone. I am warning you, before you start, that the "pattern of this world" means that you are always doing what you want and never what you need. The "renewing of the mind" is a new approach to everything that you have done in the past. Take a moment to think about the last habit that you were successful at starting. What was your mindset? Trust me, going on this journey will not be easy, but it will be beneficial.

Transforming the Mind

Reflection Question:

What have been your thoughts about money?

What will improving your finances provide?

Action Items:

List the ways that changing your mindset about money will impact your financial habits.

Prayer:

Father God, I give my mind over to you. I ask that your Holy Spirit help me to develop a healthy, positive mindset regarding my finances. In Jesus' Name, Amen.

DAY 4: CLEAN YOUR EYES

Why do you look at the speck of sawdust in your brother's eye and pay no attention to the plank in your own eye?

Matthew 7:3

It is time to look at the plank in your eye.

The last time you went to your doctor's appointment, whose symptoms were discussed? Did they discuss Susan from room one or Matt from last week? Nope. They talked about you. Gaining financial freedom is a personal journey, not a judgement opportunity. At the end of the day, you are the only person responsible for making your financial decisions. I, also, have some other news for you. Talking down about another individual does not make your bills go away. Judging others so you can feel better about your current position is not needed. I need you to place blinders on your eyes and focus on yourself only. Yes, encouragement from others may be needed. Accountability is necessary. But in the end, you are the one required to put in the work. Let's get ready to face the shadow of your decisions that follow you wherever you go. Concentrate on you and no one else.

Clean Your Eyes

Reflection Question:

Rate your current financial status: poor, fair, good, excellent. Explain your reasoning.

Action Item:

Look in the mirror. Be honest with yourself. Write down the worse financial decision you have made. Now say the prayer and forgive yourself. God has forgiven you.

Prayer:

Lord God, forgive me for the judgement that I've placed on myself and others. Open my eyes to the financial decisions I've made. Help me to see the areas where I need your correction and guidance. In Jesus' name, Amen.

DAY 5: LOOK AT YOUR CIRCLE

Don't put your confidence in powerful people; there is no help for you there.

Psalm 146:3

As iron sharpens iron, so one person sharpens another.

Proverbs 27:17 (NIV)

If I were to tell you that your circle can determine your success, would you believe me? One of the hardest lessons that you will learn during this financial journey is that everyone is not going to want you to succeed. Everyone is not going to be happy that you are changing financially because your financial decisions will undoubtedly affect other areas of your life, including friendships. Deciding who is for you and who is against you is very important to improving your finances. Is there someone in your circle that is negative about money any time it is mentioned? Or do you have a friend that continues to urge you to shop after you have said you are cutting back? Be careful of who you allow on your journey. Surround yourself with people who will hold you accountable with your new financial decisions.

Look at Your Circle

Reflection Question:

Do the 2-3 people you spend the most time with have good financial habits?

Action Item:

Identify an accountability partner to connect with you on your journey to financial freedom.

Prayer:

Heavenly Father, give me a keen sense of discernment. Allow me to connect with individuals that encourage me to walk in your perfect will. In Jesus' name, Amen.

DAY 6: THE GAME CHANGER

Bring the whole tithe into the storehouse, that there may be food in my house. Test me in this," says the Lord Almighty, "and see if I will not throw open the floodgates of heaven and pour out so much blessing that there will not be room enough to store it.

Malachi 3:10 (NIV)

A lot of people discuss tithing as if, if you do not give the full ten percent, you are not giving correctly. I think differently, only because of experience. I have learned that God isn't as concerned about the amount as He is about the heart. Yes, ten percent is the standard, but there is more behind that. In the New Testament, Jesus shares about a woman who gave her last and how she had given more than the rich (See Mark 12:41-44). Jesus is, later, quoted in Acts 20:35b saying, "It is more blessed to give than to receive." Again, the percentage is not mentioned. In Day 1, we discussed that we are "Trusting God's Way" … that means ALL of His way. God has requested that we give, not because he needs it, but because he knows that giving will improve who we are as a people. When you have the right heart, you are thinking of yourself less, and he will bless you for it. I know there may be some of you who say, "I do not have any money to give." That is okay! God is not superficial. He will not condemn you if you do not have any money. You may be wondering, What else can I do? Are you volunteering your time? Do you dedicate time to read His word? God honors that as well. Whatever commitment that you decide (and stick to), God will bless your small piece and multiply it well beyond your imagination (Ephesians 3:20).

Trisa's Truth:

Personally, I started with 3 percent fresh out of college. Why? That was the number I gave God, and after prayer, he never said no. I gave consistently, and God has blessed my finances to where there is no way I would not give to him. I get excited as the number keeps rising. Now, I am working on giving 10 percent gross. It has truly been a journey, but I am so grateful that God blessed my little effort. If he can do it for me, I know he can do it for you. Trust God with what you give, and he will take care of the rest.

The Game Changer

Reflection Question:

Are you giving God a tithe?

Action Item:

If you are not tithing, would you be willing to commit to give God, at least, 1 percent (net or gross) today? Test him and see how he will bless the remainder.

If you truly believe you cannot afford to give anything at the moment, commit yourself to acts of service to God and watch him bless you, so you can continue to give in service and, eventually, monetarily.

Prayer:

God, I know it is more blessed to give than to receive. Increase my faith by accepting my commitment to tithe to you today. Bless it so it may be used to help the growth of your kingdom and bless those in need. In Jesus' name, Amen.

DAY 7: CHASE YOURSELF, NOT OTHERS

Each one should test their own actions. Then they can take pride in themselves alone, without comparing themselves to someone else, for each one should carry their own load.

Galatians 6:4-5

On Day 5, I asked you to check your circle. Today, I'm asking you to check yourself. The one person that you should never be able to catch up with is yourself. Why? Each day, you are striving to become a better version of yourself. That means that tomorrow's version of you is a product of today's actions. Do not get caught up in the perception of others' success. We do not have the privilege of living anyone else's life. Truthfully, if we were to catch a glimpse of everything that it took to get them to this point, we may want to run in the other direction. Instead, I encourage you to chase the biggest competition out there…YOURSELF. If you need something to dig into, reflect on your growth. Are you further along today than you were one year ago, two years, etc.? I know it is tough, in our social media society, to not get caught up in the success of others. However, wasting time on someone else's effort keeps you in the same place. So let's get ready to chase future you!

Trisa's Truth:

My family is filled with teachers. So many, that, in high school, many of my teachers assumed I would go into teaching as well. While I respect the profession, it was never my desire to teach in a K-12 setting. I did end up teaching, but not the way anyone expected. If I would have followed the path of everyone around me, I do not know if you would be reading this book right now. Chasing yourself, also, means that you are chasing what you were designed to do, not what others think you are supposed to do.

Chase Yourself

Reflection Question:

Have you dreamed about your life five years from now?

Action Item:

Write down your dream life five years from today. (Dream big!) Now let's chase it!

Prayer:

Lord, provide me with blinders to stay focused on myself throughout this journey. I know that my timeline may be different from those around me. Remind me frequently of my progress and what I am moving toward. In Jesus' name, Amen.

DAY 8: EMBRACE THE JOURNEY

Let perseverance finish its work so that you may be mature and complete, not lacking anything.

James 1:4

Have you ever tried to learn something new? I'm referring to something you really do not have much familiarity with. If you're like me, you start Googling up a storm to try to figure out how to do this task. Finally, you discover some YouTube video that gives you a step-by-step guide to complete the task. The expert on the video makes it look so easy. Then, you try, and it is much harder than it looked and likely very frustrating. You end up either giving up or trying to "patch,'" as my mom calls it, and say that is good enough.

Money can be viewed similarly because, at its core, it's adding, subtracting, multiplying, and dividing. However, the application may not be that cut and dry. Yes, balancing a checkbook should be as simple as applying an elementary math education, but you may still find yourself getting frustrated with the adding, subtracting, multiplying, and dividing. In the words of my middle school math teacher, Mrs. Gordon, "The calculator is only as smart as its user." As we transition to the next phase of this devotional, you will learn tools that you can apply to shift your mindset. They will not be complicated, but it will take perseverance to get to the dream life you just wrote yesterday. Developing good, healthy money habits is not a get-rich-quick scheme. There will have to be work involved. Every day you are successful in completing the "easy" tasks, you are positioning yourself one step closer to a greater future.

Embrace the Journey

Reflection Question:

Do you think you are doing a good job of completing the easy task? What do you need to work on?

Action Item:

Write down the mindset you would like to have during this journey. Think of what you would tell yourself on a day when you are struggling. Place this somewhere you can revisit whenever it is needed.

Prayer:

God, I understand this will not be a huge change overnight but small steps at a time. Give me the strength to endure this journey as I embrace YOUR way and not my way. In Jesus' name, Amen.

DAY 9: KEEP IT SIMPLE

But his officers tried to reason with him and said, "Sir, if the prophet had told you to do something very difficult, wouldn't you have done it? So you should certainly obey him when he says simply, 'Go and wash and be cured!'" So Naaman went down to the Jordan River and dipped himself seven times, as the man of God had instructed him. And his skin became as healthy as the skin of a young child, and he was healed!

II Kings 5:1-14 (NLT)

People think there is this complex formula for fixing their finances. We have been told that we have to sign up for this program or do something extreme. I, however, am reminded of the story of Naman. He was told by the prophet to dip himself seven times into the water to be healed of his leprosy. He didn't want to do it because it wasn't complex. We are that way when we talk to God about our finances. We ask for extravagant miracles while he asks us to do something simple. It could be to cut back on eating out. It could be to pick up a few more hours at work. It could be to start writing down your expenses. Getting your finances in order is a lot of simple tasks stringed together. It isn't complex. However, you must be willing to do these simple steps repeatedly.

Keep It Simple

Reflection Question:

Do you think that it will take a lot of hard tasks to fix your finances? Why or why not?

Action Item:

Pick one goal for this year. Now create an action plan using worksheet 2.

Prayer:

God, please show me what I can do today to improve my finances. I accept your instructions, no matter how small the task. In Jesus' name, Amen.

DAY 10: USING YOUR TALENT

And I was afraid, and went away and hid your talent in the ground. See, you have what is yours.

Matthew 25:25 (NASB)

In the Bible, Jesus taught in parables (earthly stories with heavenly meaning). In Matthew 25: 14-30, a man gave a different amount of talent (money) to three people. He told them, "Take care of this until I come back." Two of the three were able to work the money and have more when the man came back. The last person had buried the talent and said, "Here. I did what you said. I kept it for you."

What does this have to do with anything? God has each given us a life, skills, and a brain. We have been equipped to do great things, but what are you doing with what God has given you? Are you trying to improve? Are you trying to enhance your capabilities? Or are you just content with where you are currently? God is challenging you to do better. He has so much in store for us. But you have to be ready to work. Are you ready to work with what God has given you?

Using Your Talent

Reflection Question:

Do you think you have done a good job of using your talent? Why or why not?

Action Item:

Write down your talents. If you are uncertain, ask 3 people who know you well to help you identify them.

Prayer:

God, please show me my talent. Holy Spirit, give me insight on how to best use my talent for God's glory. I do not want to bury the gifts you have provided. Show me what I am hiding that may help myself and others. In Jesus' name, Amen.

DAY 11: THE KEY - DISCIPLINE

No discipline seems pleasant at the time, but painful. Later on, however, it produces a harvest of righteousness and peace for those who have been trained by it.

Hebrews 12:11

Discipline is that word that we hear repeated many times when it comes to change. I personally have heard it the most when referencing an athlete and their workout regimen. You can exchange the word *discipline* with the word *consistent*. Are you doing what needs to be done over and over? Are you repeating the same task? One may say they lack discipline. You are either consistently doing the right thing or consistently doing the wrong thing? It is a matter of your perspective on the matter. For the past few months, I have been following Dr. Caroline Leaf, a neurologist studying the human brain in response to change. I'm not a scientist, but here is my interpretation. Every time we choose to make better decisions, we create new brain cells that weaken our bad decisions. I was completely blown away by this thought pattern. (You should check her out on YouTube. It is very fascinating.) Each day, we have the opportunity to decide how we will approach life. By repeating the process of deciding to strive for improvement, we change how we operate. In the end, we will reap a harvest that is worth it all. Read the verse again. It is not going to be pleasant. It is going to produce something that is much greater than your current state. It will give you peace. So it will be worth it all.

Trisa's Truth:

Discipline is definitely something I struggle with, but this began to change the moment I started sharing my struggles with my accountability partners. It has become easier for me to stick to my goals. I had to stop keeping my struggles a secret. That is why I can be so honest in this devotional.

The Key - Discipline

Reflection Question:

What financial area(s) do you struggle with most and need more discipline in?

Action Item:

Decide on and implement one way that you can work towards increased discipline.

Prayer:

Lord, show me where I need to have discipline. Help me to be honest with myself and others, so I am able to make the changes needed to improve my finances. Give me courage. In Jesus' name, Amen.

DAY 12: ANT MENTALITY

Go to the ant, you sluggard!

Consider her ways and be wise

Proverbs 6:6

Have you ever paid attention to how the ant and the grasshopper operate? Grasshoppers destroy everything in their path, while ants store up for the winter. Ants are natural savers, while grasshoppers want everything immediately. There are two ways to have extra money: 1) Create or earn extra income, or 2) spend less. Under most circumstances, you may not be able to create extra income, but you can consume less. How do you do that? You have to learn your personal habits. In the worksheet I have provided for you, you will be able to track your spending habits. I want you to track every penny spent throughout the rest of this devotional. You will be able to see "where is your treasure."

Ant Mentality

Reflection Question:

Where do you think you spend the most money?

Action Item:

Use the "Track Your Expenses" worksheet throughout the remainder of this devotional.

Prayer:

Lord, help me to see where I spend the majority of my money. If there is space to reduce my spending, give me the wisdom to make the changes. In Jesus' name, Amen.

DAY 13: TWO SIDES OF DEBT

Do not withhold good from those to whom it is due, when it is in your power to act. Do not say to your neighbor, "Come back tomorrow and I'll give it to you"—when you already have it with you.

Proverbs 3:27-28

Suppose one of you wants to build a tower. Won't you first sit down and estimate the cost to see if you have enough money to complete it?

Luke 14:28

Debt! I have not met one person in my life who enjoys debt in their personal life. It can be very crippling when you think about it. You are essentially renting to own that particular possession. It can be especially scary if you're in a position in which missing one paycheck could throw everything off. I know it's hard to face this part, but if you are going to experience true freedom in your finances, it is necessary to discuss the good, bad, and ugly parts of finances. I selected these two verses to discuss your past and your future. The verse in Proverbs is your charge to take care of anything that is in your name. You are responsible for it, and you must pay it. Pretty straight forward. However, this devotional is more about the future than the past. What do we need to do moving forward? We really must take time to decide if you can afford a debt or not. Today's action items are things you should do before taking out any additional debt. Understanding what you can really afford is one of the great benefits of healthy finances. In order to do so, you have to know what debt is in your name. Your action item today will require you looking up your credit report. This is not your score, but everything that has your name attached to it.

Also, if you are really serious about this process, you should really limit or not take out any debt until everything is paid off.

Two Sides of Debt

Reflection Question:

Does your debt make you feel overwhelmed?

Action Item:

1. Pull your credit report from the 3 credit bureaus (TransUnion, Equifax, Experian)

   a. 3 ways to pull your report

      i. Visit www.annualcreditreport.com
      ii. Call 1-877-322-8228
      iii. Complete this form.
         https://www.consumer.ftc.gov/sites/www.consumer.ftc.gov/files/articles/pdf/pdf-0093-annual-report-request-form.pdf

2. Complete this formula

$$\% \ of \ income \ paid \ to \ debt = \left(\frac{Total \ monthly \ minimum \ debt \ payments}{Gross \ income}\right) x100$$

Note: Use worksheet 4 to get find your total monthly minimum debt payments. Gross income is your pay without any taxes taken out.

3. If this number is below 20%, you are in a healthy place and should be able to afford the debt.
4. If it is above 20-34%, you may be in danger. If it is 35% or over, you should not take out any additional debt.
5. Always consider your monthly expenses. This does not include utility bills or day to day expenses. Taking on additional debt is an obligation you should not take lightly.

Prayer:

Lord, help me to look in the mirror at my finances. Also, Lord, help me to make better decisions in the future by helping me to understand what I can or cannot handle. In Jesus' name, Amen.

DAY 14: WRITE THE VISION

And then God answered: "Write this. Write what you see. Write it out in big block letters so that it can be read on the run. This vision-message is a witness pointing to what's coming. It aches for the coming—it can hardly wait! And it doesn't lie. If it seems slow in coming, wait. It's on its way. It will come right on time.

Habakkuk 2:2 (MSG)

I'm going to be honest. This is probably one of the things I struggle with the most. I hate writing down goals. I know why; it holds me accountable. As soon as I write it down, I have the obligation of working on whatever the item is. I end up rolling my eyes at myself a few times, but in the end, it is worth it. We are 42 percent more likely to achieve our goals if we write them down, according to a study done by Dominican University in California. Here are a few of the things I have written down in the last year: I will start a financial coaching business (Done). I will workout more consistently (Done). I will read God's word consistently. As of November 18, 2018, I have only missed reading the Bible ten days this year. There are other things I can tell you about, but I'm sure you get the point. Writing the goals down allows me to meditate on them frequently. Wishful thinking does not lead to success; actions do. Writing these items down keeps you focused on the task at hand. It is, also, important to write down the why. Knowing why in many ways is more important than the what. Statement: I want to save money. Good statement: I want to save money, so I am not living paycheck to paycheck. Better statement: I have a fear of not being able to pay my bills. I never want to come home and find that I am not able to turn on the lights. I really want to get my finances in order, so I will never have to be concerned about the lights not turning on. This last statement you just read is what keeps me going. I never want my bad decisions to be the reasons why I am unable to take care of life's necessities. It drives me to help others, too.

Write the Vision

Question:

Why is getting your finances in order so important to you?

Action Item:

Go back to Day 7 and review your dream life in five years. Now write down where you will be after year 1, 2, 3, and 4.

Prayer:

Lord, please allow me to see my vision. Reveal what you would like me to see. Lord, I thank you for allowing me to write down my vision. In Jesus' name, Amen.

DAY 15: TODAY, NOT TOMORROW

Don't put it off; do it now! Don't rest until you do.

Proverbs 3:6 (NLT)

You are probably noticing a theme. I think it is safe to say that waiting until tomorrow is not a solution in my book. It is what separates you from the crowd. You ever tried a New Year's resolution. How many times have you stuck to it? Any start of a major change in my life has not occurred on January first. A resolution, by definition, is a definite decision. The skills and tools that I have provided are not meant for you to wait until you finish reading. You are to start now. Waiting twenty-four hours or a week can mean the difference between you getting the house you want in the future or just missing out on it. Think about it. Opportunities come up all the time. We will say, "I wish I had the money to do x, y, and z." If you start today, maybe you will be able to do the things that you enjoy sooner rather than later.

Today, Not Tomorrow

Reflection Question:

What are you going to do today to improve your finances?

Action Item:

DO IT TODAY! If you haven't started already, begin your action plan.

Prayer:

Lord, do not let me put off the things that I can do today. Remove the procrastination mindset from my life, so I can tackle the challenges that come my way. In Jesus' name, Amen.

DAY 16: IT DOESN'T WORK UNLESS YOU DO WORK

Whatever you have learned or received or heard from me, or seen in me-put it into practice. And the God of peace will be with you.

Philippians 4:9 (NIV)

God has been very gracious to give us free will. He has also been gracious to give us the tools and the skills to do what is needed. But you can read as many books as you would like. You can get advice with Jesus tapping on your shoulder. However, if you do not put the advice into action, none of this matters. God helps us as we move in the right direction. Yes, he will provide us with grace, but he challenges us to be better. This entire section has been about the tools that are needed to go in the right direction. Now it is up to you to utilize the things that have been provided. I promise that, when you start to show that commitment, God will provide you with the peace that is needed to endure. You know the saying, "You can lead a horse to water all day, but you can't make him drink it." Are you going to drink the water, or will you remain thirsty?

Trisa's Truth:

This is not about finances, but it is definitely applicable. I personally have struggled with my weight for a very long time. I lacked the energy to handle the responsibilities I had in my life. So I finally stopped complaining and started working out. In 2018, I lost twenty pounds by committing to working out for 200 days. I have put in work, and it has paid off. And it has helped me in other areas. I see my commitment to working out, and I am able to commit to other things as well.

It Doesn't Work Unless You Do

Reflection Question:

Here is a moment for you to reflect. Have you ever read a self-help book but never did any of the suggestions? If so, why not?

Action Item:

Ask someone close to you the following question: Do I have a history of saying, "This time I'm going to change?" Do you believe me when I say it? Note: Encourage an honest answer. Sometimes, we need to hear the truth.

Prayer:

God, I pray that I am able to put the action behind my words. Lord, continue to provide me with the encouragement that is needed to keep going, even when I don't feel like it. In Jesus' name, Amen.

DAY 17: ARE YOU INTENTIONAL?

Be very careful, then how you live—not as unwise but as wise, making the most of every opportunity, because the days are evil.

Ephesians 5:15-16

In each week, we have 168 hours. Each day we live, we have an opportunity to try again. In this faith in finances journey, you will have to intentionally decide to make the right choices. How do you need to be intentional? I decided on a budget of $30/week to eat out during the month of November. It has been tough. The result is, I haven't eaten out on the weekend all month. The reward is, my budget remains intact. Making these types of decisions will be necessary. This is a great way to bring in your accountability partner. Let them know what your goals are and how you plan to achieve them. You have to follow up. If they aren't following up with you or vice versa, what is the point of telling each other your goals? As you write down your visions and goals, revisiting them is essential to your success.

Trisa's Truth:

In December 2017, I started letting two of my friends know my goals in multiple areas of my life (Spiritual, Financial, Health, Business, and Music Ministry). At first, it was weird to tell them my status weekly, but over time, it has really helped because I have to tell someone I'm trying to make progress. I don't want to waste their time, so I do the work.

Are You Intentional?

Reflection Question:

What goal would you like to accomplish over the next month?

Action Item:

Write down your intentional action items and let your accountability partner know. Set up a date and time to let your partner know your status, at least, two times a month.

Prayer:

Lord, help me to be more intentional in my walk as I improve my bad money habits. Let me not forget my goals. In Jesus' name, Amen.

DAY 18: RESPONDING TO PROSPERITY

As surely as I live, declares the Sovereign Lord, your sister Sodom and her daughters never did what you and your daughters have done. "Now this was the sin of your sister Sodom: She and her daughters were arrogant, overfed and unconcerned; they did not help the poor and needy. They were haughty and did detestable things before me. Therefore I did away with them as you have seen.

Ezekiel 16:48-50 (NIV)

There will come a point that you will be doing better financially in the future. Bills will be paid. Money will be in your savings account. You will be doing the things that you love more than the things you hate. It will be an awesome feeling. But I must warn you, we have a civic responsibility not to forget those who are in need. This passage of scripture talks about a community that had EVERYTHING, but they were not willing to help the needy. If you go back to Genesis 13-14, you will learn that Sodom was destroyed because of their style of living. Remember me discussing the secret ingredient of giving? I'm repeating it again because it is that important. God has equipped those of us who are thriving to help those who are suffering. I would not challenge you to give away all your possessions. However, it is important to do your part. Hoarding your money does not do anyone any good. There is not one charity that is the perfect for everyone. But there is something that is perfect for you. Find something that you are passionate about and commit to it. Pay it forward. Being the person who never gives is not a good look for anyone. Once you have made it, don't forget how and where you started.

Responding to Prosperity

Reflection Question:

If you had the opportunity to give to any cause, what would it be?

Action Item:

Write out a plan on how you would give to this organization if you had the means today.

Prayer:

God, I thank you in advance for the blessings that you will provide for my life. Show me where I can make an impact in my community and in this world by giving back. In Jesus' name, Amen.

DAY 19: BALANCE IS THE KEY

The second is this: "Love your neighbor as yourself." There is no commandment greater than these.

Mark 12:31 (NIV)

I love flying. I will say this, airlines are very consistent in their preparation for its passengers. If you have never been on a plane, let me give you a quick rundown. After everyone is seated, the flight attendants will give a demonstration. They will tell you, in case there is an emergency, an oxygen mask will release above your seat. If you see someone needing assistance, please secure your mask first before helping them. This is dedicated to my servers out there. You will bend over backward to help someone in need. When someone calls for a request, your answer is, usually, "yes," even when you know you have other priorities. I'm here to tell you that "no" is now an acceptable response. In yesterday's devotion, I told you to not forget the needy. In this one, I'm telling you not to forget yourself. With time, you will develop this tool. My coworkers and I have this running theme going on within our conversations. "What is your best yes?" It has been extremely helpful in seeing situations in a different light. At this point, you may be saying, "What does this have to do with money?" You cannot show love unless you have taken care of yourself. The scripture says, "Love your neighbor as yourself." Are you neglecting yourself to help others? A good way to help this problem is to budget your giving. If you know how much you have available to give, you do not set yourself up to fail.

Balance is Key

Reflection Question:

Have you ever neglected your own well-being to get someone else out of trouble?

Action Item:

Write down a list of things that you will not compromise on.

Prayer:

Lord, help me to see my needs, so I am able to help others. I realize that, if I lack energy, I am no good to anyone. Help me to learn when to prioritize me. In Jesus' name, Amen.

DAY 20: LETTING GO

Get rid of all bitterness, rage and anger, brawling and slander, along with every form of malice. Be kind and compassionate to one another forgiving each other, just as in Christ God forgave you.

Ephesians 4:31-32

By this time, you should have realized that much of our conversation has been about yourself, more than others. I do agree that there are outside factors that do play a role in your finances. Ultimately, it is you who has taken the journey you have traveled. I have great news for you today. You can be forgiven. There is no reason to hold on to the hurt, pain, frustrations, or anger of your past mistakes. Today is a new day, and you have been provided with the opportunity to move forward. If you do not know Christ as your Lord and savior, I want to tell you about him. He died a long time ago, so we wouldn't have to carry the burden. He died, so we do not have to be ashamed of our past. Most importantly, he died, so we can have eternal life. Our lives become a testimony. Our lives can be a gift to someone else who is struggling with the same issues that we have today. So forgive yourself. Each time you let go, a layer of your past is removed, and you are able to achieve your next goal. Imagine a timeframe now where you are able to share your journey and say, "I remember when…." Get ready to start on a great journey of taking care of the things that God has provided you, one decision at a time. Get ready to live the best version of your life.

Trisa's Truth:

I have beaten myself up so many times in the last fourteen years. There are many decisions that I wish I could get a do-over on, but unfortunately, that is not the case. I have had my share of bad decisions since leaving the security of my parents. I have had the drops in credit scores, a car payment that I could not manage, and moving out on my own a little too early. My favorite was during my co-op in 2007. My parents know this now by the way. I had two apartments at the time because I didn't understand subleasing. Although I was making close to $22/hour, I was broke because each of my checks were to maintain two apartments. I left my pots and pans. I had $20 to my name before my first check. I bought a cake pan, bread, eggs, and sausage. I ate breakfast for every meal for about a month. In order to look like the Joneses, I rented furniture to maintain for a week while my parents visited me. Instead of telling the truth, I struggled. That was the LONGEST five months of life. I wouldn't be able to tell you that truth if I hadn't forgiven myself. I would not be able to help you if I hadn't forgiven myself. Now to why getting ourselves together is so important....

Letting Go

Reflection Question:

What is something that you have been holding on to that you need to let go of? What do you need to forgive yourself for?

Action Item:

You remember that dream life you have written down? Go back and read it again. Now, write a letter to yourself today as if your dream life has happened.

Remember that feeling. This is what you are pursuing … peace.

Prayer:

Lord, thank you for letting me know that my past is forgiven. Help me to move forward and find the peace needed, so I can not only help myself but be a blessing to others. In Jesus' name, Amen.

DAY 21: WHAT IS YOUR INHERITANCE?

A good man leaves an inheritance to his children's children, But the wealth of the sinner is stored up for the righteous.

Proverbs 13:22

Webster's Dictionary says that an inheritance is "the condition of the past generation." So what is the current condition of your generation? Will your possessions allow your children to build a house? Or are you providing them with termites that will require pest control? We should prepare to give our children a foundation that will provide provision, not hardship. Doing renovations on yourself will prevent your child from having to clean up your mess. Grieving is a natural part of life, but it should not come with baggage. Getting your finances together not only helps you, but it helps your family, too. You are working on something that is greater than yourself. The condition of your current generation should, also, include knowledge. Throwing your child out into the world without any skills is setting them up for failure. Maybe they cannot know every detail of the family struggles. But you can explain how much groceries cost at a minimum. They should, also, have a savings and checking account before they leave home. This will allow them to understand how a bank operates. Teach them principles that can be applied easily, instead of learning through hardships.

Trisa's Truth:

I do not have kids, but I do have family who are younger than me. My responsibility is to them. When the opportunity presents itself, I give them knowledge to prepare them. I encourage their questions and even challenge their thoughts. My niece earned $20. When I asked her if she was paying her tithe, she had a look of shock on her face. I said, "You can't give God $2, and you get to keep $18." She said, "Oh, that's it? I can do that." See that small moment of showing her the priority to God planted a seed.

What is Your Inheritance?

Reflection Question:

Have you thought about the inheritance that you will leave behind? If so, what is it? If not, what will it be?

Action Item:

Find one lesson that you can teach your child (or a child connected to you) this week, no matter how small.

Prayer:

Lord, I thank you for allowing me to write this devotional and use my life to share what you have provided me. Lord, I pray for blessings over the person reading this right now. May they be able to start on a journey of trusting you and seeking your guidance with their finances and every area of their lives. Lord, give them the wisdom to make the right decisions for their family that will carry them for generations to come. May they be blessed by their obedience to you. I thank you and praise you. In Jesus' name, Amen.

BONUS DAYS

When I started writing this devotional, I was convinced that twenty-one days would be a stretch. You may have felt the same way. However, it looks like we've both made it! I'm excited about your progress, so much so that I threw in an additional week of devotionals! I believe that these additional days will be added fuel on your journey. Don't stop now. You're well on your way to financial freedom!

DAY 22: IT IS THERE WAITING

[35] Jesus went through all the towns and villages, teaching in their synagogues, proclaiming the good news of the kingdom and healing every disease and sickness. [36] When he saw the crowds, he had compassion on them, because they were harassed and helpless, like sheep without a shepherd. [37] Then he said to his disciples, "The harvest is plentiful but the workers are few. [38] Ask the Lord of the harvest, therefore, to send out workers into his harvest field."

Matthew 9:35-38

I am a country girl, born and raised in south Alabama. Each summer, my granddad would wake us up at 6:00 AM to pick peas. Man, I hated it! We were supposed to be sleeping in and hanging around the house. The rules were pretty simple. Pick the peas and shell them before your mom gets home from work. So we would truck it over to the garden by my uncle's house and pick the peas. Afterward, we would shell them. Does not really sound like a lot of fun. There are two lessons I have learned from this recurring summer routine.

Life Lesson 1: You have to start early and often before it gets hot. Getting up early gave us the rest of the day to ourselves. Once I started playing, I was never told to stop because I'd taken care of business first. The same is true with money. Make the right decisions early, and you will be able to enjoy everything that you want later. No one will be able to tell you to stop.

Life Lesson 2: There is enough for everyone. We picked the peas until our hands were dirty. Each of us had a row. I never had to worry about not filling my bucket. The work is required for everyone. Maybe a person has a larger salary, but the principles are all the same. It may have taken me longer because I was six and my cousins were teenagers, but I got the same reward at the end — freedom to plan the rest of my day. You, too, will get the same freedom if you put in the work.

The harvest is plentiful. The rewards are plentiful, but there are not enough people who are willing to do the work. Let's do the work, so we can reap the rewards of the harvest.

It Is There Waiting

Reflection Question:

Are you willing to do the work to succeed? Be honest. What excuse has kept you from working? What will you do to correct that?

Action Item:

Name one skill you have learned from your family that has shaped how your view work.

Prayer:

Lord, I realize this will be hard work. Thank you for letting me know that there is enough available for me and everyone in my circle. I understand that my path may be different, but I must stick to my path and not others. In Jesus' name, Amen.

DAY 23: BEST FOR YOU

Hebrews 11

The entire chapter of Hebrews is called "the hall of fame of faith." It lists multiple people in the Old Testament. Some of the list includes Noah, Abraham, Moses, Samson, and David. Each person in this passage of scripture is noted for their faithfulness. Faithfulness is the similarity, but their paths were different. Each played a very significant role in how we view faith today. None of them were given the instructions in the exact way. The only requirement is to trust God. I have given you a few tools through this devotion. You are not required to use them. They are only suggestions. I am a nerd. I love Excel spreadsheets and apps on my phone to make life easier. That may not work for you. If you are a pen and paper person, that is fine. At the end of the day, you have to find out what works best for you and be comfortable with that. God may not tell you to do it the exact way prescribed in this devotional. At the end of the day, go back to the Father and seek counsel. We were are all uniquely made, so make the decisions that are unique to you.

Best for You

Reflection Question:

Have you ever tried to make someone else's way work, instead of trusting your instincts?

Action Item:

If you are a visual person, create a vision board.

If you are a verbal person, write down five affirmations to repeat daily.

Each of these items should be looked at daily.

Prayer:

Lord, I know the directions you will give me will be different from what you give others. Lord, I accept the directions you have given me and trust you know what is best. In Jesus' name, Amen.

DAY 24: CELEBRATE THE JOURNEY

This is a day you are to commemorate; for the generations to come you shall celebrate it as a festival to the Lord—a lasting ordinance.

Exodus 12:14

There will be a lot of work during this journey, but there will also be a lot of success. In the passage above, God was about to complete the last plague on Egypt, which led to them out slavery. God has ordered them to celebrate their freedom. In the same way, you should celebrate the journey. You should be able to reflect often and understand that you do not look like what you have been through. Why? It is the perfect motivation. You can say, "Wow! I remember when I didn't have any savings when I had a flat tire. Now, I have enough money to buy a whole set if needed." YES! Embrace your progress because it will keep you going. Even tell your progress because it will be motivation to someone else. If they can do it, so can I.

Trisa's Truth:

I drive a pretty decent car now. During and after college, I had a hand-me-down. It was paid for and got me to work. Unfortunately, it was man-made, so it died. Toward the end, I had to pump the gas before I cranked it. I put water in each morning. I drove with the windows down because the AC caused the car to smoke up. I kept a jug of water in my car, just in case. The back window didn't couldn't come down, so I got my brother-in-law to take the motor out. But I loved that car! There will be times when you are not "where you want to be," but that is not a reflection of where you're heading. Keep pushing. One day, you will be able to tell a horror story, too, and see how far you have come.

Celebrate the Journey

Reflection Question:

Have you ever celebrated progress? What does that look like for you?

Action Item:

Set a reminder three months, six months, and one year from today. It should be titled "How far have I come in the last...."

Prayer:

God, I thank you for establishing a standard to see our progress. Lord, I am so grateful that I do not look like what I have been through. Help me remember those times and moments of struggle and frustration with gratitude for your grace. In Jesus' name, Amen.

DAY 25: IS GIVING UP AN OPTION?

*Do you not know that in a race all the runners run, but only one gets the prize?
Run in such a way as to get the prize.*

I Corinthians 9:24

*Let us not become weary in doing good, for at the proper time we will reap a harvest
if we do not give up.*

Galatians 6:9

Is giving up an option? The short answer is no. The long answer is still no. Life is a journey of ups and downs, even when we are not trying. So you might as well be working toward something that is worthwhile. Have you really paid attention to what it has taken for you to get this far? Maybe you are someone who is desperately trying to take care of your family. For the last year, you have worked multiple jobs to make ends meet. Even though you may come tired each night, you still get up at the crack of dawn to provide for your family. Anyone who is single, exchange family for yourself. You have no one to fall back on, so you don't take many off days. Because guess what? If you can't go to work, the bills will not get paid. Does any of this sound familiar? Each of us are at different crossroads in our lives. It will take sacrifice, determination, perseverance, grit, and faith to achieve our goals. Quitting keeps you from your goals, hurts your family, and hurts yourself. The only person you can control in this life is yourself. If you are reading this today and think that you should give up, I want to remind you of one thing. Today is going to pass. If you work on today, tomorrow will be better. There is a song called "Increase

My Faith" by Brian Wilson. The chorus says, "On days when it's hard to believe, increase my faith." You got this! Keep going and DO NOT QUIT! It is worth the work.

Is Giving Up an Option?

Reflection Question:

Why isn't quitting an option for you?

Action Item:

Write a note to yourself that you can use on your most frustrating day.

I will start it off.

I will not quit because…

Prayer:

Lord, thank you for letting me know that I am not a quitter. I know that you have equipped me with everything I need to keep going in this race. Increase my faith. In Jesus' name, Amen.

DAY 26: IT WILL TAKE SACRIFICE

To do what is right and just is more acceptable to the Lord than sacrifice.

Proverbs 21:3

My mom used to give us instructions during the summer while she was at work. She would tell us, "While I'm at work, I need you to clean the bathroom, living room, and kitchen." Later, she might have called and said, "Take the chicken out of the freezer." When she came home, if we had only done three of the four things, she would be irritated. I can hear her now. "You didn't do what I said." Now this didn't happen often because there were four of us, so the duties were split. Isn't that the trick we try to play with our finances? I didn't go out to eat this week, but I did go to the mall and buy something that could have waited. I did tithe this week, but when someone asked me for help, I said no, even though I had the extra money. A partial right is still wrong. Doing things the right way is what is pleasing to God. He doesn't want your almost effort. He does provides us with grace and understands that we are a work in progress. However, God also expects us to grow in maturity and strive to be better. Sacrifice and delayed gratification are basically the same thing. You should be willing to sacrifice temporary pleasures for long-term benefits. Saying "no" to eating out and "yes" to saving will prepare you for retirement. Saying "no" to reckless spending and "yes" to budgeting will reduce anxiety. You aren't saying "no" to yourself. You are saying "yes" to making yourself better.

It Will Take Sacrifice

Reflection Question:

How do you need to say "yes" to making yourself better? What do you need to say "no" to in order to make yourself better?

Action Item:

Name one "reckless" spending habit that needs to be improved.

Name one good spending habit that you can grow.

Prayer:

Lord, show me where I am not being obedient to the process and provide me with wisdom to do things the right way. In Jesus' name, Amen.

DAY 27: WALL OF JERICHO

Joshua 6

Quick Bible lesson:

Joshua is now the leader for the Israelites. Moses is dead. God told Joshua, "Jericho is yours. This is what I need you to do. Walk around the exterior once a day for six days. On day seven, I need you to walk around seven times while the priests are blowing the trumpets. When the people hear the trumpets, they need to shout as loud as they can and the wall will collapse." Growing up, this story sounded kind of ridiculous. A shout will make a building fall down? Really? It wasn't until I was in college that I realized this really could happen. I was at a football game. It was the Florida game at Bryant-Denny. This was the second year for Nick Saban. I do not think I have ever been in a place so loud. And I could literally feel the stadium shaking under my feet. Why am I telling you this story? God asked them to be silent for six days without making a sound. You do not have to tell everyone what you are doing. Yes, your accountability partner is necessary, but shouting to the world is not necessary. Work in silence with consistency. God is doing amazing things in the background that you cannot see. Everyone does not need to know what is going on. Shouting to the world prematurely opens the doors for negative comments and distractions that you do not need.

Trisa's Truth:

I moved back to Tuscaloosa in 2013. I got an email from my former professor. She wanted to meet with me. I did not think anything of it. I'm paraphrasing, but the conversation went something like this. The professor asked if I had ever considered teaching. At the time, I didn't know that a master's degree was the requirement to teach adjunct at UA. I had earned my master's because I wanted to help people, but I never thought I would be an instructor. I was completely floored. With this professor's help and guidance, I applied and taught eight semesters at the University of Alabama. I have taught 120 students, give or take, on personal finance. All of this was done in silence. You do not know where your obedience will lead you.

Wall of Jericho

Reflection Question:

What does your patience look like?

Action Item:

An impulse purchase is when you buy something out of emotion. For your next impulse purchase, see if you can wait seventy-two hours before getting that item.

Prayer:

Lord, thank you for working in the background. Lord, let me know when to tell and when to be quiet. May my journey be like the battle of Jericho and may the troubles of my life be destroyed with obedience. In Jesus' name, Amen.

DAY 28: COMMUNICATION

Words kill, words give life; they're either poison or fruit—you choose.

Proverbs 18:21

It has been a long day, and when you come home, your spouse has purchased a new car, a new TV, an expensive piece of jewelry, or a bag full of clothes. There is only one problem. You didn't know. So you begin to argue about whatever was purchased. Eventually, your spouse apologizes, and everything is better. You eat dinner, watch TV, and go to bed. The next morning, you are going to get your cup of coffee, and what do you see? The new car out the window, the TV in the living room, the jewelry on the dresser, or the bag of clothes still sitting in the chair. You are irritated all over again. This is what a lack of communication can do to your family.

Being on the same page with your spouse is vital to any type of success. Money disputes lead to a good portion of divorces. Lack a communication is a big part of that. It is vital that you and your spouse be on the same page. Singles, I am not excluding you from this conversation. Each person should have a clear understanding of what they value, in regard to their finances. If you don't understand what you believe, how can you explain to someone why you are mad? Take time to really express to yourself what values you believe with your possessions. This will make it so much easier to explain when the conversation comes up. To each spouse reading this, I pray and hope that you and your spouse have the same feelings in regard to improving your finances. I realize that it may have been difficult in the past to bring up the conversation. I hope you don't give up. As you go through this journey, you will learn more about yourself. You will be able to explain your "WHY." Hopefully, it will give your spouse insight into why it is important to you and open the doors of communication, so you both can move toward your financial goals.

Communication

Reflection Question:

How often do you check in for desired purchases?

Action Item:

Pick a check in time with you and your spouse to go over future purchases every three months. (Three months is not a mandatory time. You know your family.)

Prayer:

Lord, I pray that you give me the guidance to communicate with my spouse about our finances. Prepare me and my spouse to be open to communicate. I pray that we learn to listen to understand so that we may move forward in doing what is best for our family. May the words of my mouth be acceptable. In Jesus' name, Amen.

THINGS TO REMEMBER

1. Trusting God with everything means EVERYTHING.
2. You cannot focus on the long-term goal without working on the short-term goal.
3. Mistakes are going to happen. Just keep going.
4. There is value in having someone with you on the journey.
5. Giving is the key that unlocks everything.
6. Focus on your journey, not others.
7. Fixing your money will require you to work.
8. Great communication will reduce arguments.
9. Be sure to recognize your milestones.
10. Be sure to teach your children (or those who you influence).

WORKSHEET APPENDIX

Worksheet 1 Dream Out Loud

Day 7

What is your dream life five years from today? Date: __/__/__

Note: Feel free to be as detailed as possible.

_____

_____

_____

_____

_____

_____

_____

_____

What is your status approaching your dream year 4? Date: __/__/__

Note: Feel free to be as detailed as possible.

_____

_____

_____

_____

_____

_____

_____

_____

What is your status approaching your dream year 3? Date: __/__/__

Note: Feel free to be as detailed as possible.

_____

_____

_____

_____

_____

_____

What is your status approaching your dream year 2? Date: __/__/__

Note: Feel free to be as detailed as possible.

_____

_____

_____

_____

_____

_____

_____

_____

What is your status approaching your dream year 1? Date: __/__/__

Note: Feel free to be as detailed as possible.

_____

_____

_____

_____

_____

_____

_____

_____

Worksheet 2: Action Planning

Day 9

Note: Defining how you achieve a goal will increase your chance of success. You can repeat this for any goal.

What is my goal?

_____

_____

_____

_____

What will I do DAILY to accomplish this goal?

_____

_____

_____

_____

What will I do WEEKLY to accomplish this goal?

_____

_____

_____

_____

What will I do MONTHLY to accomplish this goal?

_____

_____

_____

_____

What will I do YEARLY to accomplish this goal?

_____

_____

_____

_____

Worksheet 3: Expense Tracker

Track your expenses over the next two weeks. Find out where your treasure is by your bank account. Although this is a very simple format, this is a great place to get started.

Date	Vendor/Store	Description (What is it for?)	Amount

Worksheet 4: Debt Calculator

List of your debts

Now that you have pulled your credit report. It is now time to list all your debts. Also, include any debts that you owe individuals that will not show on your credit report

https://www.creditkarma.com/calculators/debtrepayment

Debt Name	Minimum Payment	Balance	Due Date

Worksheet 5: Budget Prep Sheet

Budget Prep Sheet

In order to prepare your budget, you need to have a list of all your expenses. This should be referenced each time you prepare a budget.

List of your Monthly and Occasional Expenses

Name of Expense	Due Date	Average or Minimum Payment

82

Worksheet 6: Budgeting 101

Here are the basic steps to completing a budget that can get you started.

1. Based on your income
2. Complete each pay period or when funds are received
3. Done in same location (Notebook, Excel, YNAB) with list of expenses (Worksheet 5)
4. Repeat

Note: Repeating the budget process is the most important step. Each pay period is different, but the steps are the same. It will probably take longer initially, but with application, it will get better. This is a very basic budget to use from your worksheet 5. I have entered tithes and savings for you. You should plan until the remaining income is 0.00. This is your plan.

Pay Period

From: __/__/__   To: __/__/__

Income: _____

Expense	Amount	Remaining
Tithes		
Savings		

Worksheet 7: Prosperity Plan

Day 19

List organizations and causes that you would like to support with your blessings. You are blessed to be a blessing to others.

Name of Organization

_____

_____

_____

Why this organization?

_____

_____

_____

What can you do today to help this organization?

_____

_____

_____

_____

_____

What would you like to do in the future?

_____

_____

_____

_____

_____

CONGRATULATIONS & NEXT STEPS

Congratulations! You have just completed the first days of your Financial Freedom Journey! You are well on your way to living the best version of your life. Each decision that you make, from here on out, will affect you both now and later. The beauty in that is that it doesn't have to be negative.

This book is just the beginning of a larger movement. Hopefully, the last few weeks have really helped you shift your mindset and habits toward Financial Freedom. Send me an email to join my mailing list and be among the first to know about the book launch. My goal is to help individuals one thought, one action, and one habit at a time. You are a part of that vision.

If you haven't already, please take the time to connect with me on Facebook and Instagram (@PughFC). I want you to have access to my live trainings, previous recordings, and a community of others looking to enhance their lives on the Financial Freedom Journey. I, also, welcome your feedback on what the last few weeks have meant to you. Send me an email about your experience to pughfinancialcoaching@gmail.com.

Excitedly,

Latrisa Pugh

ABOUT THE AUTHOR

Latrisa Pugh holds a Bachelor's in Accounting and a Master's in Consumer Science with a focus on Financial Planning. For more than eight years, she has worked as an Accountant for the Alabama Department of Corrections and University of Alabama. Latrisa lends her financial expertise to the surrounding community through the provision of financial literacy services for youth and organizations. As the founder of Pugh Financial Coaching, she offers tailored instruction on money management to help individuals and families learn to live the best version of their lives. Since 2013, Latrisa has dedicated more than 1,200 hours to teaching financial literacy throughout Alabama and internationally. Latria's personal interests include a love for music and a growing commitment to physical health. Latrisa resides in Tuscaloosa, Alabama. ROLL TIDE!

PUGH FINANCIAL COACHING

Pugh Financial Coaching Offers the Following Services:

Teach Me to Budget Course

Individual Coaching

Group Coaching

Speaking & Training

Visit Our Website TODAY to learn more and book the start to your
Financial Freedom Journey

https://pughfc.com/

Made in the USA
Monee, IL
27 February 2020